Read-About® Geography

New York City

By David F. Marx

Consultant
Linda Cornwell, Learning Resource Consultant,
Indiana Department of Education

CP Children's Press®
A Division of Grolier Publishing
New York   London   Hong Kong   Sydney
Danbury, Connecticut

Visit Children's Press® on the Internet at:
http://publishing.grolier.com

Designer: Herman Adler Design Group

Library of Congress Cataloging-in-Publication Data

Marx, David F.
 New York City / by David F. Marx.
  p. cm. – (Rookie read-about geography)
 Includes index.
 Summary: An introduction to New York City, its people, and famous sights.
 ISBN 0-516-21552-3 (lib.bdg.)   0-516-26558-X (pbk.)
 1. New York (N.Y.)—Juvenile literature. [1. New York (N.Y.)]
 I. Title. II. Series.
 F128.33.M37 1999   98-37342
 974.7`1—dc21   CIP
                                                    AC

New York City is one
of the world's biggest cities.
More than seven million
people live there. They are
all called "New Yorkers."

Much of New York City sits on islands. Around the city are these bodies of water: the Atlantic Ocean, the Hudson River, the East River, and the Long Island Sound.

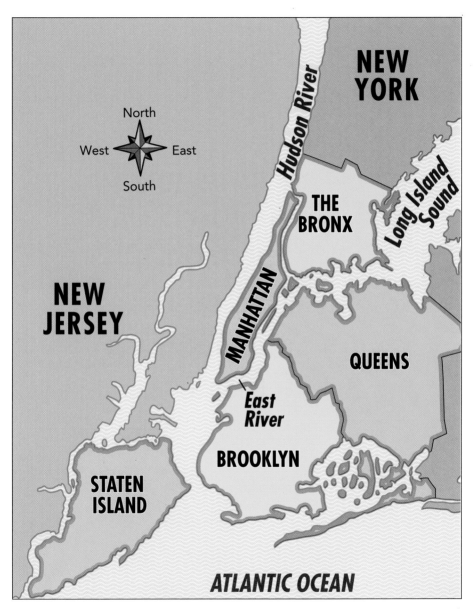

The city is made up of
five separate parts called
boroughs (BUR-ohs)—
Brooklyn, the Bronx,
Manhattan, Queens,
and Staten Island.

Manhattan is the smallest borough.

But it is home to most of New York's famous sites.

9

10

In Manhattan, you can ride to the top of some of the tallest buildings in the world!

The Empire State Building is 1,250 feet tall.

It was the world's tallest building when it was built in 1930.

Even taller are the two towers of the World Trade Center.

They each stand 1,350 feet high.

13

Macy's Thanksgiving Day Parade

If you visit on Thanksgiving, you can see the Macy's Thanksgiving Day Parade.

Or you can play in Central Park, one of the world's largest city parks.

Central Park

There are a lot of fun things to see and do outside of Manhattan, as well.

Travel to the Bronx and visit the animals at the Bronx Zoo.

17

18

In Brooklyn, ride the
Cyclone roller coaster
at Coney Island.

This amusement park is
more than one hundred
years old.

All of New York's boroughs are home to many different kinds of people, including Chinese, Jewish, Italians, Polish, Hispanics, and African-Americans.

21

A brownstone apartment building

Some families live in houses. But New York is so crowded that most people live in apartment buildings.

Brooklyn is famous for its brownstone apartment buildings (named for their brownish-red bricks).

A lot of New Yorkers don't own cars. They can take a train or a bus to almost anywhere in the city.

Some trains are subways, which run in tunnels underground.

People riding the subway

The Staten Island Ferry

Some people even ride a boat to work! You can ride a ferryboat to get to Manhattan from Staten Island.

And to get to Manhattan from Brooklyn, you can walk across the Brooklyn Bridge.

The Brooklyn Bridge

As you cross the bridge, you'll see one of New York's most famous sites. The Statue of Liberty stands on a tiny island in New York Harbor.

"Lady Liberty" has welcomed people to New York City for more than one hundred years. She'll welcome you, too, if you come to visit!

Words You Know

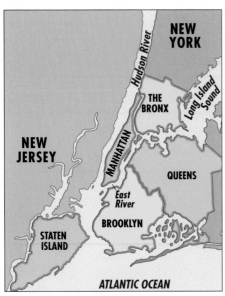

boroughs

Bronx Zoo

Brooklyn Bridge

brownstone

Central Park

ferryboat

Empire State
Building

roller coaster

subway

Statue of Liberty

World Trade Center

31

Index

About the Author

David F. Marx is an author and editor of children's books.
He resides in Connecticut.

Photo Credits

Photographs ©: Gamma-Liaison: 22, 30 bottom right (Phoebe Ferguson), 25,
31 middle right (Porter Gifford), 18, 31 middle center (Carolyn Schaefer), 26,
31 top right (Allen Stephens); H. Armstrong Roberts, Inc.: cover (J. Blank), 29,
31 bottom left (J. Blank), 9 (P. Degginger), 7 (R. Kord); Monkmeyer Press: 10,
31 middle left (Bopp), 15, 31 top left (Goodwin), 3 (Montaine); Rigoberto
Quinteros: 27, 30 bottom left; Tony Stone Images: 13, 31 bottom right (Jon
Ortner); Woodfin Camp & Associates: 17, 21, 30 top right (Bernard Boutrit),
14 (A. Ramey).
Maps by Joe LeMonnier.